BEHAVIORAL FINANCE

WHAT EVERYONE NEEDS TO KNOW®

BEHAVIORAL FINANCE

WHAT EVERYONE NEEDS TO KNOW®

H. KENT BAKER, GREG FILBECK, AND JOHN R. NOFSINGER

OXFORD

UNIVERSITY PRESS

OXFORD
UNIVERSITY PRESS

Oxford University Press is a department of the University of Oxford. It furthers the University's objective of excellence in research, scholarship, and education by publishing worldwide. Oxford is a registered trade mark of Oxford University Press in the UK and certain other countries.

"What Everyone Needs to Know" is a registered trademark of Oxford University Press.

Published in the United States of America by Oxford University Press 198 Madison Avenue, New York, NY 10016, United States of America.

Library of Congress Cataloging-in-Publication Data
Names: Baker, H. Kent (Harold Kent), 1944– author. | Filbeck, Greg, author. | Nofsinger, John R., author.
Title: Behavioral finance : what everyone needs to know® / H. Kent Baker, Greg Filbeck, John R. Nofsinger.
Description: New York, NY : Oxford University Press, [2019] | Includes index.
Identifiers: LCCN 2018019087 (print) | LCCN 2018020904 (ebook) |
ISBN 978–0–19–086875–8 (UPDF) | ISBN 978–0–19–086876–5 (EPUB) |
ISBN 978–0–19–086873–4 (pbk. : alk. paper) |
ISBN 978–0–19–086874–1 (hardcover : alk. paper)
Subjects: LCSH: Finance—Psychological aspects. | Investments—Psychological aspects. | Investments—Decision making.
Classification: LCC HG4515.15 (ebook) | LCC HG4515.15 .B339 2019 (print) |
DDC 332.601/9—dc23
LC record available at https://lccn.loc.gov/2018019087

1 3 5 7 9 8 6 4 2

Paperback printed by LSC Communications, United States of America
Hardback printed by Bridgeport National Bindery, Inc., United States of America

CONTENTS

2. Cognitive Biases   41

3. Emotional Biases and Social-Cultural Influences   77

4. Investor Behavior   99

5. Nudge: The Influence of Frame Dependence   127

6. Cognitive Ability   163

PREFACE

Who Are the Authors?

H. Kent Baker, CFA, CMA, is University Professor of Finance at the Kogod School of Business, American University, where he served as the Chair of the Department of Finance and Real Estate and headed the Finance Center of Excellence. Before joining the faculty at American University, he held both faculty and administrative positions at the business schools of Georgetown University and the University of Maryland. Professor Baker has consulting and training experience with more than 100 organizations and is a former President of the Southern Finance Association. He has published more than 175 refereed journal articles and written or edited 32 books, including several on behavioral finance, among them *Behavioral Finance: Investors, Corporations, and Markets* and *Financial Behavior: Players, Services, Products, and Markets*. His book *Investor Behavior: The Psychology of Financial Planning and Investing* received the 2015 USA Best Book Award in the Business: Personal Finance/Investing category. *Investment Traps Exposed: Navigating Investor Mistakes and Behavioral Biases* (2017) was the 2017 Book Excellence Award Winner in Personal Finance and the Bronze Medalist, 2018 Axiom Business Book Award in Personal Finance/Retirement Planning/Investing. He has received numerous awards for research, teaching, and service including the University Scholar/Teacher of the Year. Professor Baker has a BSBA (management) from Georgetown University; an MBA (finance), MEd (educational administration), and DBA (finance) from the University of Maryland; and an MS (quantitative methods), MA (training and career development), PhD (educational administration and organizational development), and PhD (counseling and student development) from American University. In his spare time, he is a professional musician who plays five instruments and has recorded and toured.

Greg Filbeck, CFA, FRM, CAIA, CIPM, PRM, holds the Samuel P. Black III Professor of Finance and Risk Management at Penn State Erie, the Behrend College and serves as Director of the Black School of Business. He previously served as Senior Vice President of Kaplan Schweser and held academic appointments at Miami University (Ohio) and the University of Toledo, where he also served as the Associate Director of the Center for Family Business. Professor Filbeck has authored or edited eight books and published more than 95 refereed academic journal articles. Professor Filbeck conducts consulting and training worldwide. He currently serves as President of the CFA Society Pittsburgh and was previously the President of the CFA Society Toledo and the Southern Finance Association. He received the Impact on Practice Award from the Black School of Business in 2015, the outstanding teaching award among iMBA faculty in 2010 and 2012, and the Penn State Behrend Regents award for Outstanding Researcher in 2011, and was the 2013 recipient of the Penn State Behrend Outstanding Outreach Award. He has a BS (engineering physics) from Murray State University and an MS in Applied Statistics from Penn State University and holds a DBA (finance) from the University of Kentucky. Filbeck is a Professionally Registered Parliamentarian, is a qualified administrator of the Myers-Briggs Type Indicator, and has 12 years of experience in radio broadcasting.

John R. Nofsinger is the William H. Seward Endowed Chair in International Finance at the College of Business and Public Policy, University of Alaska, Anchorage (UAA). Before joining the faculty at UAA in 2014, he was a professor at Washington State University and held the Nihoul Faculty Fellow from 2008 to 2013. He also held an assistant professor appointment at Marquette University. Professor Nofsinger has authored or coauthored 11 finance trade books, textbooks, and scholarly books. His books have been translated into 11 languages. His book *The Psychology of Investing* is in its sixth edition and is popular with investment advisors. As one of the world's leading experts in behavioral finance, Professor Nofsinger is a frequent speaker on this topic and others. He is also a prolific scholar who has published 64 articles in prestigious scholarly journals and practitioner journals. He is most widely known in the area of behavioral finance, but is also widely known for the topic of socially responsible finance. Professor Nofsinger is often quoted or appears in the financial media. He received a BS (electrical engineering) from Washington State University, an MBA from Chapman University, and a PhD (finance) from Washington State University. In his spare time, he competes in Ironman triathlons.

Why Did We Write This Book?

We are longtime friends and have worked together for years editing books and writing articles. We all completed doctoral programs in finance and learned the principles and paradigms of standard finance. For much of our adult lives, we have been fascinated by the psychology of investing and market behavior. After years of studying and researching how market participants and markets behave, we became increasingly aware of the limitations of standard finance. Although standard finance does a good job explaining how people and markets should behave based on a set of restrictive assumptions, it often fails to adequately explain how normal people and markets actually behave. Behavioral finance offers another perspective that complements the traditional finance view.

During its early years, behavioral finance identified both behavioral biases and a myriad of anomalies that contradicted accepted theoretical predictions. However, it often did an incomplete job of explaining how investors and others could deal with these anomalies or mitigate biases. Behavioral finance has been revolutionizing economics and finance at the highest levels. This is well illustrated by the world's most prestigious prize, the Nobel Memorial Prize in Economic Sciences, being awarded for behavioral topics in recent years, starting with Daniel Kahneman and Vernon L. Smith in 2002, Robert J. Shiller in 2013, and Richard Thaler in 2017. Because much of the behavioral finance research is difficult to grasp by people not directly involved in the topic, we took this opportunity to help them gain such an understanding. This book is our attempt to identify not only what everyone needs to know about behavioral finance but also what they want to know about this captivating subject. Of course, only readers of this book can determine whether we have accomplished this goal.

What Is the Book About?

Before the emergence of behavioral finance, standard finance was the reigning paradigm in academic finance. Although standard finance provides many useful insights, it offers an incomplete and unrealistic picture of actual, observed behavior. For example, standard finance assumes that people are rational and financial markets are efficient. *Market efficiency* refers to the degree to which stock prices and other securities prices reflect all available, relevant information. If financial markets are efficient, the world becomes a simple place. If people always act rationally, then security prices would fully reflect the available information and investors would be unable to consistently beat the market. If this situation were true, the vast resources devoted to analyzing, selecting, and trading securities would be a waste of time and effort.

Yet, during the past several decades, substantial research evidence has shown that people are far less rational in their decision-making than initially assumed. Casual observation also supports this fact. Just ask yourself, "Do I always behave rationally when making economic or financial decisions?" If you are being honest, the answer is no. Further, such irrational behaviors are neither random nor senseless but instead are systematic and predictable. People often repeat the same cognitive mistakes because of how their brains work. Emotions and social-cultural influences also affect behavior. For example, the human brain often processes information using shortcuts and emotional filters that influence financial decision-makers in a seemingly irrational manner. Such behavior is pervasive in investor decisions, financial markets, corporate managerial behavior, and elsewhere. The impact of these suboptimal financial decisions has ramifications for personal wealth, the quality of life, and market efficiency. For example, evidence supporting a myriad of anomalies challenges many of the tenets of standard finance. An *anomaly* is evidence of behavior that contradicts an accepted theoretical prediction.

Given that everyone makes systematic mistakes in their decision-making processes, why not develop new strategies, tools, methods, and policies to help make better judgments and improve overall well-being? This objective is where behavioral finance enters the picture. The intent of behavioral finance is not to explain rational or irrational behavior, but to explain "normal" behavior. Behavioral finance offers an alternative view of behavior and financial markets that complements standard finance. As Dan Ariely noted in his book, *Predictably Irrational: The Hidden Forces That Shape Our Decisions*, "Wouldn't economics make a lot more sense if it were based on how people actually behave, instead of how they should behave?" Given both the breadth and depth of behavioral finance, the intent of this book is not to be all encompassing.

Trying to do everything for everyone is likely to be unproductive. Instead, the book's scope is more narrowly focused. Its main purpose is to discuss how behavioral finance primarily affects individuals, especially investors, not corporate managers, institutional investors, or policymakers. However, it also notes that behavioral finance offers evidence that appears anomalous from the efficient markets perspective and offers new predictions. This focus is justified given the considerable amount of evidence that documents the biases and associated problems with individual investor trading and portfolio allocations. The book's focus should be particularly appealing to those interested in learning how behavioral finance can help to explain their behavior and improve their financial decision-making.

Behavioral Finance: What Everyone Needs to Know offers a balanced explanation of the broad issues associated with behavioral finance in a succinct but authoritative manner. It follows a straightforward question-and-answer format that should be understandable to a diverse audience. The book is organized into six chapters, each containing questions relating to each chapter's focus. The format enables browsing for topics of interest without reading the book from cover to cover.

Whom Do We Want to Thank?

Not surprisingly, many people played important roles in bringing this book from the conceptual stage to final publication. Of course, the many researchers and writers who provided insights about behavioral finance over the past four decades serve as the foundation of this book. The reviewers of our initial book proposal offered valuable comments about the most important topics to include. Our partners at Oxford University Press performed at a highly professional level throughout the entire process. Dave Pervin (Senior Editor) offered detailed comments on our draft, suggested how to frame our presentation, and nudged us in that direction. Hayley Singer (Editorial

Assistant) did an admirable job in paying close attention to the many details necessary in moving the book along. Special thanks also go to Rajakumari Ganessin (Project Manager), Richard Isomaki (Copyeditor), Leslie Johnson (Production Editor), and Claudie Peterfreund (Indexer). Linda Baker merits special thanks for proofing the entire manuscript. We also recognize the support provided to us by our respective institutions: the Kogod School of Business at American University; the Black School of Business at Penn State Behrend; and the College of Business and Public Policy at the University of Alaska, Anchorage. Finally, we thank our families, to whom this book is dedicated: Linda and Rory Baker; Janis, Aaron, Andrea, Kyle, and Grant Filbeck; and Anna Nofsinger.

BEHAVIORAL FINANCE
WHAT EVERYONE NEEDS TO KNOW®

1

FOUNDATIONS AND PSYCHOLOGICAL CONCEPTS

Historically, those traveling the financial highway were taught to follow a single route. Travelers were told that as long as everyone faithfully followed directions and weather conditions were ideal, the road would be their best choice and they would get to their intended destination. Over time, however, some became disenchanted with the journey because the highway provided a bumpy ride due to ruts in the road and often failed to get them where they really wanted to go. Some adventuresome pioneers decided to bypass the old road and to build a new one. Although they initially encountered obstacles and resistance in forging a new path, they persisted in their endeavor and eventually attracted others to help them pave the way. These pioneers, called behaviorists, created a fork in the financial highway. As Yogi Berra, the famous baseball player and coach once said: "When you arrive at a fork in the road, take it." Unfortunately, strong commitment to existing paths and paradigms can obscure one's vision of promising alternatives.[1] A *paradigm* is a standard, perspective, or set of ideas. That is, a paradigm is a model or a way of looking at something. Not surprisingly, finance traditionalists were anxious about the entrance of behaviorists into the financial highway. Although many still travel the old road, the new road has attracted numerous travelers by offering an appealing choice with very different scenery along the way.

This simple story sets the stage for two major branches in finance: the well-established standard finance and the more recent behavioral finance. Standard finance rests on classical decision theory and presumes that individuals, institutions, and markets are rational. On average, these individuals are unbiased and maximize their own self-interests. Any errors that market participants make are uncorrelated and thus are unable to affect market prices. This approach assumes that people have internally consistent preferences, access to perfect information, can apply unlimited processing power to any available information, and make optimal choices by using expected utility theory to maximize the benefit they receive from an action, subject to constraints. This book does not focus on standard finance. Instead, it discusses the foundations of the new financial highway called behavioral finance.

What Is Behavioral Finance?

Behavioral finance is a relatively new and expanding field that has exploded in popularity, especially since the 1980s. It is not only interesting but also provides important insights into human and market behavior. The precise definition of behavioral finance is still debated, partly because this discipline is constantly evolving. For the purposes of this book, *behavioral finance* is the study of the influence of psychology and other disciplines on the behavior of financial practitioners and the subsequent effect on markets.[2] Additionally, behavioral finance focuses on applying psychological and economic principles for the improvement of financial decision-making.[3]

Although initially criticized by advocates of standard finance for encroaching on their territory, behavioral finance has become part of mainstream finance for the media, investment industry, and academics. In fact, several researchers in behavioral finance and experimental economics have received the Nobel Memorial Prize in Economic Sciences, including Daniel

Kahneman and Vernon L. Smith in 2002, Robert J. Shiller in 2013, and Richard Thaler in 2017.

Behavioral finance tries to explain how people make economic decisions by combining behavioral and cognitive psychological theory with conventional finance and economic theory. In fact, behavioral finance is exhibited each time a person makes a financial decision. Research on behavioral biases—cognitive, emotional, and social-cultural—helps to explain errors in economic decision-making and to predict the behavior, especially the mistakes, of others, thus enabling them to guard against making similar errors in the future. However, the term "behavioral bias" must be used with caution because some behavioral biases can have positive outcomes.

Behavioral finance has evolved dramatically from what some considered a "pop science" and a collection of anomalies and biases to an explanation of financial phenomena. In a noninvesting context, an *anomaly* is a strange or unusual occurrence. Thus, anomalous behavior contradicts an accepted prediction or deviates from the common rule. In a behavioral context, *market anomalies* refer to situations when a security or group of securities performs contrary to the notion of efficient markets. As a result, they provide evidence that a given assumption or model does not hold in practice. Although some market anomalies are transient relations that disappear, others occur repeatedly. Theoretically, market anomalies should neither occur nor persist, but some do.

The cross-disciplinary nature of behavioral finance helps to clarify why people make the money choices they do, not dictate how they should make those choices. Behavioral finance has also revolutionized the way people think about what makes humans "tick" concerning money and why and how markets might be inefficient. However, this field of study is just beginning to understand the influences of human behavior as applied to individuals, firms, groups, or institutions making financial decisions.

Why Is Behavioral Finance Important to Practitioners?

Practitioners such as investors, financial planners and advisors, portfolio managers, corporate executives, among others, need to understand behavioral finance for several reasons. First, behavioral finance helps to explain various phenomena involving money and markets and to solve persistent problems and limitations previously addressed with the concepts of standard finance and classical economics. Evidence involving individual behavior often does not coincide with the predictions of traditional theories. However, the existence of anomalous evidence does not constitute proof that existing paradigms are necessarily "wrong." Behavioral finance offers a new set of explanations of anomalies and empirical regularities. According to Brooke Harrington, a noted financial researcher, "Learning about common cognitive errors in economic decision-making . . . feels like getting a peek inside the flawed machines that are our brains, making it seem possible to predict the behavior (particularly the mistakes) of others, and guard against them in oneself. In short, behavioral finance seems to offer insight and a sense of control, imposing order on what otherwise appears chaotic and unpredictable."[4]

Second, behavioral finance provides insights that help overcome the constraints of many traditional theories and models that rest on the belief that market participants act in a rational wealth-maximizing manner. Making this assumption severely limits the ability to make accurate or detailed predictions. Although normative models provide a basis for understanding some "idealized events," they fail to explain certain real-world events where people apparently behave irrationally and unpredictably. In other words, theoretical models try to simplify complicated things, but often do a poor job of explaining a messy real world inhabited by humans. Behavioral finance tries to fill the void between theory and practice by combining scientific insights into cognitive reasoning with conventional economic and financial theory. Behavioral finance provides a new body of theories and a new set of predictions that help to explain financial behavior and real-world markets. In doing so, it complicates the study of finance because the focus now turns to how people actually behave as opposed to how they should behave.

Third, behavioral finance is not a replacement of standard finance. Instead, it is a companion that complements standard finance. Given the complexities associated with decision-making, neither approach independently provides a comprehensive account in interpreting choice behavior. Both traditional and behavioral research in finance can identify many predictive successes and failures in their own areas. Thus, applying alternative approaches is likely to provide a more robust explanation of complex decision-making behavior than using a single viewpoint. However, given the evidence that has emerged over the past several decades, the time may be ripe to discard or at least substantially modify some of the established paradigms of standard finance.

Fourth, behavioral finance studies have identified different behavioral biases that cause some people to behave irrationally and sometimes against their best interests. Although some behavioral biases are useful, most can lead to making costly mistakes. Behavioral finance provides a means of helping practitioners recognize their mistakes and those of others, comprehend the reasons for making these mistakes, and deal with them. Being knowledgeable about behavioral finance can help people avoid emotion-driven speculation leading to losses, and thus devise an appropriate wealth management strategy. At a collective or market level, understanding biases provides a clearer explanation of the severe rise and fall in asset prices that result in bubbles and crashes. Practitioners have a vested interest in learning about behavioral finance to make them more aware of their own decision-making processes.

What Are Some Cornerstones Underlying Behavioral Finance?

Behavioral finance theory rests on several assumptions, foundations, or characteristics. A major cornerstone of behavioral finance involves *investor sentiment*, which is a theory about how real-world investors actually form their beliefs and valuations. According to behavioral finance, people exhibit behavioral preferences, and information-processing biases preventing them from making the optimal choice. Hence, they are sometimes irrational or quasi-rational, a condition that is known as bounded rationality. *Bounded rationality* in decision-making occurs when the rationality of individuals is limited by the information they have, cognitive limitations of the human mind, and the finite amount of time they have to make decisions. Based on this view, decision-makers are *satisficers* who seek a satisfactory solution rather than an optimal one.[5]

Another assumption underlying behavioral finance is that individual errors and biases in processing information are correlated among other investors (systematic), so they don't average out at the market level. That is, even if the market contains individual biases, they don't cancel each other out to make the market, on aggregate, unbiased. This situation creates the possibility that correlated errors of investors could potentially last for long periods and affect prices accordingly, hence making markets inefficient.

In an *efficient market*, security prices reflect all available information at any point in time. In an *inefficient market*, securities such as common stocks are not always accurately priced and tend to deviate from their true or intrinsic value. Given the structure of markets, they are unlikely to be perfectly efficient, as clearly evidenced by recent asset bubbles. Although history reveals many asset bubbles, bubble production seems to have accelerated sharply. Thus, markets are not only inefficient, but also appear to be showing greater inefficiency than in the past.[6]

A cornerstone underlying behavioral finance involves limits to arbitrage in financial markets. *Arbitrage* involves a costless investment that generates riskless profits by taking advantage of mispricings across different instruments or markets representing the same security. Consider the following simple example of arbitrage. Company A's stock is trading for $50 on the New York Stock Exchange (NYSE) but for $50.10 on the London Stock Exchange (LSE). By buying the stock on the NYSE and immediately selling it on the LSE, a trader would earn a $0.10 profit per share, assuming no transaction or other costs. The trader could continue to take advantage of this arbitrage opportunity until the specialists on the NYSE exhaust their inventory of Company A's stock, or until the specialists on either exchange adjust their prices to eliminate this opportunity.

Arbitrage is critical in maintaining efficient markets because the arbitrage process keeps true values aligned with market prices. In practice, arbitrage entails both costs and the assumption of risk. Thus, limits exist to the effectiveness of arbitrage in eliminating certain security mispricings. *Limits to arbitrage* is a theory stating that prices remain in a nonequilibrium state for extended periods because of restrictions placed on funds that limit the ability of rational traders to arbitrage away the pricing inefficiencies.[7] Hence, limits to arbitrage could prevent rational investors from correcting price deviations caused by irrational investors. But in real-world financial markets, arbitrage is not close to being perfect.

Within behavioral finance, the information structure and the characteristics of market participants systematically are assumed to influence both individual decisions and market outcomes. Thus, investors aren't always rational, and markets can be inefficient.

What Is Prospect Theory and What Implications Does It Have for Choice Behavior?

Prospect theory describes how people make choices between different options or prospects that involve risk and uncertainty. Risk and uncertainty differ. *Risk* involves the ability to predict the different possibilities of a future outcome, while *uncertainty* does not. Thus, risk can be measured and quantified, but uncertainty can't. Daniel Kahneman and Amos Tversky, whom many view as the fathers of behavioral finance, created this theory in 1979 and later refined this descriptive model to reflect real-life choices, not optimal decisions, as normative models do.[8] They called it prospect theory because it is a catchy, attention-getting name. Thus, prospect theory provides an alternative to conventional wisdom as represented by expected utility theory and shows how people decide between alternatives that involve risk and uncertainty.[9] In 2002, Kahneman received the Nobel Prize for having integrated insights from psychological research into the economic sciences.

Expected utility theory provides the basis for much of standard finance theory. *Expected utility theory* involves analyzing situations where people must make a decision without knowing which outcomes may result from that decision. Hence, they are making decisions under uncertainty. According to expected utility theory, a person should choose the act resulting in the highest expected utility. *Utility* is the economist's term for satisfaction. The utility, or satisfaction, of each outcome is weighted according to the probability that the act will lead to that outcome. Evidence suggests that expected utility theory makes faulty predictions about people's decisions in many real-life choice situations. For example, expected utility theory asserts that no sane individual would play the lottery or gamble with poor odds. Yet lotteries and gambling are widespread.

Prospect theory provides the most widely accepted alternative to expected utility theory. In prospect theory, the value function has three important properties distinguishing it from the expected utility function. First, prospect theory measures value in terms of changes in wealth from a reference point, whereas a utility function measures value based on the level of final wealth. Thus, people are more concerned with changes to wealth than their long-run state of wealth. For this reason, many of the super wealthy aren't satisfied with having billions of dollars because they value how much their wealth increases more than the actual level.

Second, the value function is convex when facing losses, which reflects risk-taking to avoid loses. But the function is concave for gains, which reflects risk aversion. An individual's utility function evaluates satisfaction from the perspective of risk aversion, risk neutrality, or risk attraction. Thus, investors are both risk-seekers and risk-averters at the same time. In economics and finance, a *risk-seeker* or *risk-lover* is a person who has a preference for risk, such as casino-goers. Such individuals search for greater volatility and uncertainty in investments in exchange for anticipated higher returns. Most investors are considered *risk-averse*, meaning they prefer lower returns with known risks rather than higher returns with unknown risks. In other words, risk-averse investors facing two investments with the same expected return but different risks would prefer the alternative with the lower risk.

Third, prospect theory recognizes the asymmetry of human choices. People attach greater weight to losses than to equivalent gains in wealth. That is, losses are more painful in magnitude than a similar profit is pleasurable. *Loss aversion* refers to the tendency to prefer avoiding a loss to taking a chance on receiving an equivalent gain. People often choose to minimize losses because losses have a greater impact on their psyche than gains, even with the probability of those losses being small. Thus, loss aversion implies that the pain from a $1,000 loss is greater than the pleasure from a $1,000 gain. Kahneman and Tversky were the first to show that people experience almost twice as much pain from a loss compared to the pleasure of a similar-sized gain. Loss aversion is a problem when it leads people to go to irrational lengths to avoid taking risks. Under expected utility theory, individuals don't attach a differential weight to losses or gains.[10]

Let's look at several examples to illustrate various implications of prospect theory for choice behavior.[11] People tend to have greater interest in their relative gains and losses than in their final income and wealth. But relative gains and losses require a *reference point* or anchor, which is a point used to find or describe the location of something. According to prospect theory, the reference point determines how an outcome is perceived. The reference point is often the prior level of wealth, but it could also be the wealth of someone you know. If your relative position does not improve, then you are unlikely to feel better off, despite having an increase in wealth. For example, assume that two investors know one another. If both investor A and investor B receive a 10% return on their portfolios, neither will feel better off. However, if investor A receives a 10% return on his portfolio and investor B gets a 0% return, investor A feels much wealthier regardless of the level of his wealth.

Here is another example. According to prospect theory, people tend to be loss-averse and give greater weight to losses than to gains. To illustrate: an investor who gains $1,000 on one stock and loses $750 on another may consider this situation a net loss in terms of satisfaction, despite coming out $250 ahead. Prospect theory also explains why individuals might sell assets of increasing value (winners) too soon to secure gains and hold losing assets (losers) for too long, hoping that the value of these assets will increase. Losses cause more severe pain than the pleasure resulting from a gain of the same magnitude.

As a final example, people strongly prefer certainty and will sacrifice returns to achieve greater certainty. For instance, assume you have two options: (1) a guaranteed win of $1,000 and (2) a 75% chance of winning $1,500 but a 25% chance of winning nothing. You are apt to select the first option with a sure gain of $1,000, even though the second has a higher expected gain, computed as $[0.75(\$1,500) + 0.25(\$0)] = \$1,125$.

What Is the Disposition Effect and Why Is It Harmful to Investors?

Does the saying "Cut your losses and let your profits run" sound familiar? Although this common investment advice is intended to help people engage in disciplined investment management, many investors have difficulty following it. The *disposition effect* is a tendency to realize gains quickly and defer the realization of losses. This term is shorthand for the pre-disposition toward "get-evenitis," which is the tendency for investors to hold on to a losing investment until its price returns to the original amount at which they bought the asset.[12] People exhibit this bias when they say, "If the price would just go back to what I paid, I would sell it." Of course, that is not a convincing argument for owning that stock. Empirical studies conducted with stocks and other assets such as real estate show strong support for the disposition effect.[13] However, conflicting evidence suggests that in panics, people often sell stocks that are falling in price too quickly, thus precipitating market crashes.

Although a full understanding of the underlying causes of the disposition effect is currently lacking, especially based on rational explanations, investor psychology appears to play an important role. One explanation involves *self-justification*, which describes how, when someone encounters a situation in which that person's behavior is inconsistent with his beliefs, that person has a tendency to justify the behavior and deny any negative feedback associated with the behavior. People often have difficulty accepting and admitting their own mistakes because doing so is unpleasant and sometimes painful. Investors hate losses and are willing to gamble to avoid experiencing them, so they exhibit risk-seeking behavior by holding losers.

Another behavioral reason for the disposition effect is that investors may lack the self-control to sell a losing investment. *Self-control* refers to the ability to regulate one's emotions, thoughts, and behavior when facing temptations and impulses. Hence, investors may hold on to losing investments, hoping these investments will eventually return to their initial purchase prices. Selling the loser makes the regret of buying it in the first place feel stronger. Yet investors want to lock in gains because doing so demonstrates that they made good investment decisions. That is, selling winners evokes the pleasant feeling of pride. Consequently, investors exhibit risk-averse behavior by selling winners. Thus, investors avoid regret and seek pride. A third explanation for the disposition effect involves prospect theory, but the evidence shows mixed results.[14]

The disposition effect is harmful to investors for several reasons. First, suffering from the disposition effect can be detrimental to investors' performance and increase the chances of making bad decisions. Selling winners too soon and holding on to losers too long increases the capital gains taxes that investors pay and reduces returns even before taxes. A *capital gains tax* is a tax levied on profits an investor realizes when selling a capital asset, such as a stock, for a price that is higher than the purchase price. Investors often realize gains on their investments but don't take offsetting losses. As a result, they pay higher taxes because capital gains are based on realized gains, not on overall portfolio returns. Additionally, the stocks that investors sell (the winners) as a result of the disposition effect often outperform those that they hold (the losers). So they are holding the wrong stocks. Thus, investors need to regulate their behavior to achieve specific goals.

Second, the disposition effect can affect rational decision-making. The historical price that an investor paid for an asset such as a stock is irrelevant to decision-making because it represents a *sunk cost*, which is a cost that has already been incurred and can't be recovered. Investors should not "cry over spilled milk" because they can't undo something that has already taken place. The decision to sell or hold a security should depend on its perceived future value, not the initial purchase price. Yet investors often use the initial price as a reference point for interpreting investment performance.

Generally speaking, investors would be better off holding well-performing stocks longer and selling losing stocks sooner. Investors who engage in *momentum investing* try to capitalize on the continuance of existing trends in the market. The general idea underlying momentum investing is that once a trend is established, it is more likely to continue in that direction than to move against the trend. By holding winners longer, investors may experience momentum in which winning stocks continue to rise in price. By selling a security that has been in a downtrend sooner, investors may realize a higher price than waiting until later to sell. Academic research provides support for momentum investing.[15]

To counter the disposition effect, investors can place a stop-loss order in the market. A *stop-loss order* is an order to sell a security or commodity at a specified price in order to limit a loss. Other strategies that investors use to sell losers are to group all of the loser stocks in the portfolio and sell them all at once to "get it over with." Also, investors sometimes sell a winner and a loser together to reduce the pain of regret for the loser. Interestingly, people tend to spread out the selling of winners over time to prolong the feeling of pride.[16]

What Are Heuristics?

Have you ever made a decision based on an educated guess, rule of thumb, or common sense? If so, you have used a heuristic. Heuristics are a key theme in behavioral finance. *Heuristic* are simple, efficient rules that people frequently use to help increase the speed of making decisions and forming judgments. Strategies that provide shortcuts to problem-solving and decisions take one's personal experience into account. By using heuristics, the brain generates estimates before fully digesting the available information. This process, called *heuristic simplification*, generally gets people where they want to go but sometimes sends them off course when considering investment decisions.[17]

Within behavioral finance, heuristics relate to making financial decisions in a fast and frugal manner. *Fast and frugal heuristics* refer to simple, task-specific decision strategies that are part of a decision-maker's repertoire of cognitive strategies for solving judgment and decision tasks.[18] Decision-makers often face a set of choices with uncertainty and a limited ability to quantify the likelihood of the results. Heuristics represent mental shortcuts that enable them to focus on one aspect of a complex problem and ignore others. Consequently, by using simple rules, people can make decisions more quickly and efficiently. This practical approach to processing data does not guarantee an optimal or perfect result, but it often provides one sufficient to meet the immediate goals.

Uncertainty plays an important role in adopting heuristics. For example, investors often lack sufficient information about the future trends in security prices, so they adopt ad hoc rules to make investment decisions. Although heuristics are helpful in many situations, they can also result in poor outcomes and bad decisions. Behavioral finance recognizes that people who rely on heuristics make errors, but standard finance does not. Standard finance assumes that people make perfectly rational decisions, apply unlimited processing power to any available information, and can assign probabilities to each potential outcome. They then correctly apply the appropriate tools to reach an optimal outcome. By contrast, behavioral finance makes none of these assumptions because they are unrealistic in practice. Thus, a heuristics and biases framework serves as a counterpart to standard finance theory's asset-pricing models.

Let's examine a couple of examples using heuristics—one in everyday life and another in investments. The everyday life example involves the *authority heuristic*, which occurs when someone believes the opinion of a person on a subject just because the individual is an authority figure. The strength of the bias to obey a legitimate authority figure is a result of systemic socialization practices intended to instill in people the perception that such obedience represents correct behavior. People often apply this heuristic in matters such as science, education, and hierarchical organizations such as the military. For instance, when a scientist confirms a specific finding, laymen are likely to accept this judgment because an authority figure's statement sounds convincing. Students often believe a professor's opinion because such individuals usually possess higher degrees of knowledge on the topic.

Another example of a popular heuristic used in investing concerns buying mutual funds. Given the large number of mutual funds available, investors face a potentially complex task of deciding which fund to buy. To facilitate this process, they may decide to choose funds by extrapolating past performance into the future. For example, consider the following simple rule: Past performance is the best indicator of future performance, so select funds with the highest Morningstar ratings. The *Morningstar risk rating* is a ranking given to publicly traded mutual funds and exchange-traded funds (ETFs) by the investment research firm Morningstar. The ratings range from one to five stars: one being the poorest rank and five being the best. The problem with this heuristic is that yesterday's big winners could become tomorrow's big losers. Using past risk-adjusted performance to guide investment decisions might work in very short time periods, but there is little consistency in predictive ability beyond this short-term horizon. That is, top-performing funds typically don't continue to significantly outperform other funds over long periods.[19] Although momentum investing has potential merits if properly executed, it also involves risks.[20] Hence, buying "past winners" is a tempting but flawed investing strategy over the long term.

What Role Do Heuristics Play in Forming Judgments and Making Decisions?

People use heuristics to form judgments and make decisions for several reasons. First, they employ heuristics because their brains have a natural need for closure. Thinking is hard work. The brain uses different strategies to process information, make judgments, and solve problems. Some approaches are complex and others are quick. To decrease the amount and complexity of information requiring analysis, the brain excludes some information and uses shortcuts to simplify the process. In some instances, heuristics can actually be beneficial by enabling quicker judgments, thus reducing the time and mental effort spent researching and analyzing information to solve a problem and to control for extreme complexity. These mental processes are particularly appropriate for decision-making under uncertainly.

Second, heuristics help to avoid *paralysis by analysis*, which is the state of overanalyzing or overthinking a situation so that a decision or action is never taken, in effect paralyzing the outcome. Consider a paradox in philosophy called "Buridan's ass" that involves the concept of free will. In this hypothetical situation, a hungry donkey is placed between two bales of hay that are exactly the same distance from the donkey. Which bale of hay will the donkey choose to eat? According to the paradox, the donkey can't make any rational decision because the bales are equidistant. Thus, the donkey starves to death because of its paralysis.

Although heuristics can sometimes be helpful by saving time, effort, and energy, they often are instinctive and irrational. Using heuristics can hinder the development of new ideas and lead to systematic and predictable mistakes, causing intelligent people to make poor decisions, such as when investing. As Hersh Shefrin, who is one the first financial economists to incorporate ideas from psychologists into working theories, notes, "Because of their reliance on heuristics, practitioners hold biased beliefs that render them vulnerable to committing errors."[21]

Four general categories or types of general purpose heuristics are representativeness, availability, anchoring, and affect. The first three heuristics can lead to psychological biases and systematic errors in how people think, while the fourth relates to emotions, or how people feel. What follows is a discussion of each of these types of heuristics.

How Does the Representativeness Heuristic Influence Judgment and Decision-Making Behavior?

Let's examine a classic example by Amos Tversky and Daniel Kahneman that illustrates how the representativeness heuristic can influence perceptions of other people.[22] Assume that you perceive someone as shy and withdrawn, with little interest in people or in the world of reality. This person is tidy and meek and has a need for order and structure, as well as a passion for detail. Which of the following professions is this individual likely to practice: farmer, salesman, airline pilot, librarian, or physician? Based on the representativeness heuristic and stereotypes about these professions, you probably thought that this person was a librarian. This snap judgment about someone's occupation based on knowing about a few personality traits is likely to result in a hasty and erroneous conclusion. However, if you assessed the accuracy of at least some of the reported traits, you might have drawn a different conclusion.

The *representativeness heuristic*, also called *representative bias*, is the tendency to use past experiences or beliefs to guide the decision-making process.[23] In making quick judgments, people often compare a person, event, or object to a prototype or representative idea that already exists in their mind that they tend to view as similar or dissimilar based on how it matches up with their model. Although this heuristic is useful in making judgments quickly, it can also lead to poor choices, stereotypes, and errors because people often have a skewed belief about the past. Why? Representativeness presumes that once people or events are categorized, they share all the features of other members in that category, which plays into stereotypes of people and events. Another downside of using the representativeness heuristic is the tendency to ignore other courses of action besides the one that immediately springs to mind.

Here are two examples of representativeness in investments. Investors may prefer to buy a stock that has had abnormally high recent returns (the *extrapolation bias*) or may misconstrue a company's positive characteristics, such as producing high-quality goods, as an indicator of a good investment.[24] Let's examine the extrapolation bias a bit more. One example is when investors might be tempted to forecast a company's future earnings based on a short history of past high earnings. However, this form of stereotyping can lead to overestimating or underestimating a company's future performance because past earnings may be an inappropriate guideline for its future. Although every prospectus points out that past performance does not guarantee future results, investors often ignore this warning. A *prospectus* is a formal legal document that is required by and filed with the Securities and Exchange Commission (SEC) that provides details about an investment offered for sale to the public. Unfortunately, investors may fail to take into account that the high earnings could result from chance and be unlikely to reoccur. Or the stock's price might have already adjusted to the growth rate and thus may not be a good investment going forward. Another example is that, during the early phase of a stock market or housing bubble, market participants erroneously conclude that prices will continue to rise into the future. Similarly, when prices have been falling, investors have mental difficulty getting back into the market because this bias leads them to believe that prices will continue to fall.

If you are prone to representative bias, you can begin to lessen this tendency by being aware of the likelihood of a particular event based on situational information. You should look for ways to introduce objectivity into the decision-making process. You can also surround yourself with people who challenge your opinions and listen carefully and empathetically to your views.

What Are Two Common Biases Associated with the Representative Heuristic?

Two common biases associated with the representative-ness heuristic relate to the law of small numbers and mean reversion. The *law of small numbers* is a fallacy in which people assume that a small sample is representative of a much larger population. As a result of not considering the sample size, people often derive rules from small groups that are reliable only in much larger sample sizes.

A classic example is a coin toss. If tossing a coin results in heads, say, seven times in a row, the inclination is to predict an increase in the likelihood that the next coin toss will be tails, "evening things out." Given that the probability of a fair coin being heads or tails is 50% each time the coin is flipped, the percentages should balance out. Right? This belief is incorrect in the short run. Those probabilities can be quite skewed in small samples because each toss is an independent event unconnected to the toss before or after it.

The bias in this example, called the *gambler's fallacy*, is the belief that past events influence the future even when each event is unrelated to the previous one. This fallacy is a glitch in thinking. Those committing the gambler's fallacy expect past events to influence the probability of something happening in a game of chance. Thus, if gamblers playing games that draw numbers, such as keno, roulette, and a lottery, believe that a number is "due" because it has not been drawn lately, they would be surprised to be told that the odds have not changed.

Now let's apply the gambler's fallacy to an investment example. Assume that the Standard & Poor's 500 Index (S&P 500) has closed higher 10 trading sessions in a row. The *S&P 500* is an index of 500 stocks seen as a leading indicator of U.S. equities and is widely regarded as the best single gauge of the performance of large-cap U.S. equities. *Market capitalization (cap)* refers to the number of shares outstanding times the share price. If you believe that after 10 up days the odds of a market decline are higher, you could enter into a short sale on the SPDR S&P 500 exchange-traded fund (ETF). Before proceeding, let's explain each of these terms. *Short selling* is the sale of a security that is not owned by the seller. The short seller borrows the stock from a broker and then sells it at the current market price, with the sale proceeds credited to the short seller's margin account. The seller is motivated to enter a short sale based on the belief that a security's price will decline, enabling the seller to buy it back at a lower price to make a profit. *SPDR* is an acronym for the Standard & Poor's Depositary Receipts, now the SPDR S&P 500. An *ETF* is a type of investment fund that is traded on a stock exchange. This ETF is designed to track the S&P 500 stock market index. On a purely statistical basis, past events don't connect to future events. Although various reasons could explain a market downturn on the eleventh day, the fact that the market was up 10 days in a row is irrelevant. Although many people likely believed that increasing nine days in a row would result in a down day on the tenth day, the market actually went up that day. As previously mentioned, investors should be aware that past performance is no guarantee of future results.

Another bias associated with representativeness is the failure to allow for *mean reversion* or *regression toward the mean*, which is the reversion of outcomes toward computed averages over long periods of time. Investors often ignore the fact that extreme performance usually returns to the average. Thus, both high-performing and low-performing mutual funds— winners and losers—tend to revert to the averages over time.

An implication of such biases is that market participants are inclined to over- or underestimate the performance of stocks or mutual funds that have achieved results either above or below the market average in recent years. Stocks with better performance than the market for several years often subsequently have results that are worse than the averages. Underperforming stocks in the past often outperform in the future.

What Is the Availability Heuristic and How Can It Affect Investment Decisions?

Certain events are likely to stand out in your mind more than others. For example, after hearing a highly publicized news report about big lottery winners, you start to overestimate your likelihood of winning the lottery. Consequently, you increase your spending on lottery tickets. This real-life example illustrates the availability heuristic in which related events or situations immediately spring to mind when you are trying to make a decision. As a result, you might misjudge the frequency and magnitude of these events. You give greater importance to this information and tend to overestimate the likelihood of similar things happening in the future.[25]

Another example of the availability heuristic involves physical visibility and supermarket shoppers. Assume you are shopping for groceries. What types of products catch your attention? Evidence shows that shoppers tend to buy more products in a supermarket that are displayed at eye level or just below (more available) than those that are more out of the way (less available). The availability heuristic has the power to persuade. Consequently, supermarkets and other retailers can charge manufacturers more if they want their products displayed in these well-placed positions.[26]

The *availability heuristic*, also called the *availability bias*, is a mental shortcut that facilitates decision-making based on information that is easy to recall, widely available, and highly publicized. In other words, this heuristic allows people to judge the likelihood of an event or situation simply based on examples of similar situations that quickly come to mind, allowing them to extrapolate to the situation in which they find themselves. This relation partly happens because of the limitations on memory. Although representativeness and availability seem similar, availability is about particular examples and ease of recall, whereas representativeness is less about specific examples than about stereotypes.[27]

Although the availability heuristic can lead to fast decisions, it can sometimes result in bad judgments. Relying on this heuristic can result in incorrectly assessing the likelihood of events because decision-makers place undue emphasis on information that is readily available. People mistakenly think of things that stand out in their minds as more important in making good decisions or more likely to occur than those that are difficult to imagine or remember.[28] This ease of recall can influence behavior, thus making people predisposed to over-emphasize, overestimate the likelihood, or misinterpret this information. Factors influencing the availability heuristic on people's judgments and decisions include the ability to induce affective or emotional reactions, extremely dramatic events, and recent events.[29]

Here are several examples of the availability bias involving investments. When evaluating stocks, investors tend to over-rate the importance of recent investment news and discount older information. They also are inclined to invest in the highest-performing mutual funds (winners), which are generally the most highly advertised, due to the availability and impact of this information. Another example of availability bias involves the financial crisis of 2007–2008. Many investors left the stock market as a result of a steep decline in market prices. Their recent experience led to an upward bias in their expectations of another crisis.

Investors need to be aware that recent, prominent, and emotionally charged financial events are readily available and can often dominate their choices. To lessen availability bias, you need to retain a sense of perspective. That is, you should avoid being caught up in the latest news and short-term approaches and focus on the long-term picture. You also need to examine other tools, investment options, and decision-making strategies available to you before making a choice. By thoroughly researching your investments, you can better understand the relevance of recent news and act accordingly.

What Role Does Anchoring Play When Making Investment Decisions?

Have you ever considered buying a diamond engagement ring? If so, how much should you pay for the ring? Conventional wisdom suggests spending about two months' salary on the ring. This standard or benchmark is an example of anchoring and represents an irrelevant reference point created by the jewelry industry to increase its profits. The amount spent on an engagement ring should depend on what someone can afford, not on some arbitrary reference point.[30]

Anchoring refers to the tendency to rely on the first number or piece of information as a subjective reference point for making future judgments. Think of anchoring as a "first impression" bias. For example, in a salary negotiation, the person who makes the first offer establishes a range of reasonable possibilities in each person's mind. Once someone forms an initial picture of a situation, seeing other possibilities is more difficult. Thus, any counteroffer is a reaction to that opening offer, which serves as an anchor. Although a popular belief is that an applicant should not make an opening offer, research suggests that view is completely backward. The person who makes a first offer is often better off.

A problem with the anchoring heuristic is that people often have difficulty altering or changing their viewpoints when faced with new information. By being anchored by salient past events, they incorrectly interpret new information through the lens of the original anchor. Sometimes people make adjustments to these imperfect anchors, but these adjustments can also reflect biases.

Anchoring is prevalent in many financial decisions, including investments, and can lead to poor decisions. Here are a few examples. First, investors engaged in anchoring could reject a correct decision such as buying an undervalued investment or selling an overvalued investment. They could also accept an incorrect decision such as ignoring an undervalued investment or buying or holding an overvalued investment.

Another example is when investors latch onto the original price they paid for an asset as a reference point, such as a stock that they acquired at $50 a share. This historical price serves as an anchor. If the stock price declines, those with an anchoring bias tend to hold on to the stock until they get back the original price they paid. They have anchored their fair-value estimate to the acquisition price (a reference point) rather than to fundamentals. Thus, these investors assume greater risk by holding the stock hoping it will return to its purchase price in order to break even.

A third instance involves investing in companies whose stocks have experienced large price drops during a short period. Investors often anchor on the recent high stock price, believing that a price drop affords the opportunity of buying the stock at a substantial discount. Although price declines can sometimes enable investors to take advantage of short-term volatility, such declines often result from a worsening of the stock's fundamentals. By contrast, other investors apply a negative anchor after a market bubble bursts. That is, they anchor to a negative outcome and believe more market declines are coming.

A final example is when people anchor on investment names such as the terms *conservative* or *aggressive*. Not surprisingly, mutual funds include such descriptors. The problem is that the notion of conservative or aggressive could differ markedly between the fund's portfolio manager and its investors.

Although detecting anchoring bias requires awareness, mere awareness is not enough. Overcoming this bias requires engaging in critical thinking and reflecting on one's decision-making history. Another approach is to carefully evaluate an investment's potential by identifying the factors that underlie the anchor and replacing guesswork with quantifiable data.

What Is the Affect Heuristic and How Does It Influence Decision-Making?

Have you ever made decisions that were heavily influenced by your current emotional state? Of course you have. How did that work out for you? Emotions play a critical role in both big and little decisions that you make. Evidence suggests that when you are in a positive emotional state, you are more likely to perceive an activity as having high benefits and low risks. If your emotional state is negative, you are more inclined to see the activity as having low benefits and high risks.[31]

The psychologist Paul Slovic coined the term *affect heuristic* to describe how people let their emotions color their beliefs. An affect heuristic is a mental shortcut in which a person relies on emotion, intuition, and "gut feeling" when making a decision. This fast and frugal heuristic is quick and relatively easy to apply and reduces the cost of searching for and processing information. By contrast, the analytic, rational system of the brain is relatively slow and requires effort. Yet one's feelings and emotional state can influence perceptions and cognitions. Although debate exists about whether emotions enhance or detract from investor decision-making, the overall evidence suggests that, on balance, emotions hinder investors in making effective decisions.[32]

How can the affect heuristic influence investors? If investors have positive or pleasant feelings about something, they are more inclined to perceive an investment as having high returns and low risk. They also are apt to be more confident in evaluating investment options. For example, if investors have strong, positive feelings about a company, they are likely to perceive its stock as less risky and be willing to pay a higher price for it.[33] Hence such investors see high benefits and low risk. Why? They often generalize the good characteristics of a growth company when evaluating it as an investment. As a result, they have a habit of overestimating the likelihood of growth companies being good investments and unknowingly overpay for their shares.[34] A negative emotional state leads people to be more critical when evaluating investments.

In summary, the affect heuristic can strongly influence decisions. Being aware of the proclivity to be swayed by feelings and emotions may enable you to make more objective and clear-minded decisions in the future. Research suggests that third-person self-talks can improve emotion regulation and self-control by facilitating self-distancing and reducing ego-centric bias.[35] Hence, this strategy may prevent bad decisions in the heat of the moment by helping you to remain calm, collected, and level-headed.[36]

What Is Framing and How Can It Influence Decision-Making?

A second key theme in behavioral finance is framing. *Framing* refers to how people react to a particular choice depending on how it is presented. A *frame* is simply the form used to describe a problem or situation. Framing portrays a choice or outcome in terms of its positive or negative consequences, not as good or bad. For example, advertisers use language to frame their messages to influence consumers. They attempt to create a positive emotional frame for the product in the consumer's mind. When advertising a high-end automobile, advertisers use such words as "luxurious," "superb craftsmanship," and "well-appointed" but avoid using terms such as "expensive" and "overpriced." For a lower-priced car, advertisements employ such words as "affordable" and "dependable" instead of "cheap" and "sturdy."[37]

Standard finance assumes that describing the same content in different ways (i.e., using different frames) will not affect how people make judgments or decisions. This assumption of *frame independence* suggests that financial decision-makers view all decisions through the same objective and transparent lens of risk and return. Under the standard finance paradigm, a rational decision-maker should see through the frame, no matter how opaque. A message's framing does not change its meaning or substance, only its form. Thus, standard finance views framing as irrelevant to behavior because people should make the same decisions or have the same preferences across different presentations of the choice.

Yet much evidence suggests that this view does not accurately describe human judgment. People make different choices depending on how a given problem is presented to them. In